A Heart 4 Marriage

Dr. Luciana Philyaw Ed.D, MFT

REFERENCES

Medora, N.P, Larson, N. Hortacsu & Dave
(2000). Perceived attitudes towards
romanticism: A cross-cultural study. Journal
of Comparative Family Studies 33:150-80

Pages 17-18, 27-29

King James 1611 Holy Bible

Duhart Press LLC, the publisher

copyright 2026

Cover designed by KJB Graphic and Designs

`

DEDICATION

This journal is lovingly dedicated to my husband, Curtis Philyaw. From the very beginning, Curtis has been a living example of God's love and peace in my life. He is a hard-working man with a sincere desire to reflect God's heart not only to his family, but to everyone he encounters.

More than twenty-five years ago, when Curtis asked me to marry him, he promised me a life filled with adventure and laughter. As I look back now, I can truly say that promise has been fulfilled in ways far beyond what I could have imagined. When the Lord gently nudged me to write this devotional journal, He reminded me of the beautiful journey we have shared so far and filled my heart with even greater hope for the years still to come.

It is our prayer that these devotionals bless you as deeply as they have blessed us. We pray they encourage you to build your marriage in such a way that, if given the opportunity, you would joyfully choose one another all over again. May they remind you to build each other up, to love more deeply than you think you are capable of, and to extend grace freely.

Above all, we hope this journal serves as a reminder that you are not alone. Christ is with you, walking alongside you every step of the way, and you are supported by a community of believers who love you and stand with you as you build and nurture your marriage ministry.

Many Blessings,

Luciana

We are Stronger Together

Ecclesiastes 4:9–12

Two are better than one, because they have a good reward for their toil. For if they fall, one will lift up his fellow... And though a man might prevail against one who is alone, two will withstand him a threefold cord is not quickly broken.

What If

What is marriage? The answer depends on who you ask. Marriage and family are foundational structures in most societies, they are deeply interconnected, complex, and universal. Yet even researchers cannot agree on a single definition of marriage. Textbooks often define it as a "legally recognized contract between two people, traditionally based on a sexual relationship."

The Bible, however, defines marriage as a sacred union between one man and one woman, established by God (Matthew 19:4-6). It is a lifelong commitment rooted in faithfulness and mutual love. Christian marriage goes beyond a legal agreement; it is a covenant in which both partners live sacrificially, reflecting Christ's love for His people and the church's submission to Him. In a Christian marriage, each spouse honors and mirrors the relationship between Christ and the church.

Notice the difference between these two definitions, it's profound. Take a moment to reflect on that.

Before a couple gets married, the importance of counseling is often emphasized. Many couples take assessments such as SYMBIS, PREPARE/ENRICH, FOCCUS, or meet with their local pastors to ensure they are ready for the journey of marriage. These tools are undoubtedly valuable, but do they truly prepare you for the deeper challenge becoming *one* with another person?

Many people say that "marriage is hard work" or simply that "marriage is hard." Often, statements like these become judgments or even excuses for giving up on a relationship.

While I agree that relationships and marriages especially can be challenging at times, what if I told you they were never meant to feel overwhelmingly difficult? Marriage was designed to make life easier, not harder. At its core, it's meant to be a partnership that supports, strengthens, and uplifts both people. Let me prove it to you.

This is an example of how this book will help you build your marriage muscles. Below are study points for some, and a powerful refresher for others.

In Genesis 2:18 (NLT), the Lord God says, ***"It is not good for the man to be alone. I will make a helper who is just right for him."*** The word translated as ***helper*** comes from the Hebrew word Ezer (pronounced *AY-zer*). While our English definition of "helper" may sound like someone who simply assists, the biblical meaning is far deeper and far more powerful.

Ezer is the very same word used throughout the Old Testament to describe ***God Himself*** as our helper: ***"God is our Ezer and our shield."*** This is not a sidekick or secondary role. Ezer conveys the idea of an ally, rescuer, or deliverer someone who comes running when help is needed. An ezer is heroic.

Matthew Strong's concordance explains that Ezer can be translated as **ally or helper**, rooted in the concept of a strong support. God created woman to be an ezer to man not to serve in trivial tasks, but to stand as a powerful counterpart, a life-saving partner, and a strength alongside him.

The word *helper* (Ezer) appears twenty-one times in the Old Testament:

- 2 times to describe the woman in Eden (Genesis 2:18 and 2:20)

- 1 time to explain that Israel would offer no help to Egypt (Isaiah 30:5)

- 1 time to describe the removal of Jerusalem's prince and the scattering of his helpers (Ezekiel 12:14)

- All remaining uses refer to YHWH Himself as the Helper of His people

This alone reveals the strength, dignity, and divine intentionality in the role of the woman as Ezer.

But Scripture also gives clear guidance to the husband. In *Ephesians 5:28*, we read: ***"In the same way, husbands ought to love their wives as their own bodies. He who loves his wife loves himself."***

This verse powerfully captures the unity and oneness marriage is designed to reflect. A husband is commanded to love, cherish, and care for his wife with the same devotion he gives to his own well-being. To love one's wife is to recognize her as an inseparable part of oneself.

This teaching elevates marriage as a relationship built on:

- mutual respect

- selflessness

- deep affection

- unwavering support

- and a shared identity in Christ

Together, the biblical concepts of Ezer and self-giving love create a picture of marriage that is strong, balanced, and rooted in divine purpose.

As we move through life, we are constantly writing our own stories. Everyone we meet becomes a part of that story, and each of us is living a narrative unlike anyone else's. Together, this creates an endless range of experiences, outcomes, and choices; many of which we don't even realize we're making.

When we claim that successful or long-lasting marriages exist because the couple "worked hard," we unintentionally suggest that divorces or shorter relationships result from a lack of effort. Not only is that assumption unfair, but it also simply isn't true. And yet, the statistics around divorce make this idea feel believable enough that many young couples are choosing not to marry at all, fearing the pain of a possible divorce.

The reality is that people can pour tremendous effort into an unhealthy marriage and still end up in a situation that isn't good for anyone.

Those statements can also create the illusion that happiness in marriage is something earned only through relentless effort. But life itself is constant work by becoming self-aware, raising children, growing, healing, and learning how to be a kinder, better human being. These are the deeper labors that shape us long before we ever bring ourselves to a marriage.

Believe it or not, about 90% of what we believe about marriage is shaped by structural and cultural influences. While these forces are powerful, they do not determine everything. We still have agency, after all, Abba Father gives us choices. How we initiate, respond to, nurture, or even end intimate relationships shapes the outcomes we experience. The bottom line is that I am responsible for my own well-being and happiness. The choices and decisions I make directly influence the quality of my days and the same is true for the health and happiness of your marriage.

Consider the idea that "not to decide is to decide." Choosing not to make a decision is, in itself, a decision with its own consequences. For example, when spouses choose to have unprotected sex, a common occurrence in marriage, they are also choosing to accept the possibility of pregnancy. On a personal level, if someone decides to remain in a relationship that is going nowhere, they are effectively choosing to continue in that stagnant situation, limiting their chances of finding a healthier, more fulfilling partnership.

If you do not make a decision to work on your marriage you will become vulnerable to unhealthy choices that could damage your marriage.

Below is an assessment that will help you explore yourself and your thoughts about your marriage. Complete the assessment and make some notes.

Reflection:_____

_____

_____

_____

_____

_____

_____

_____

_____

_____

_____

_____

_____

_____

_____

_____

_____

THE RELATIONSHIP INVOLVEMENT SCALE

Take this assessment for your own records. This scale is designed to assess the level of your involvement in your current relationship. Please read each statement carefully and write the number next to the statement that reflects your level of disagreement or agreement using the following scale.

1	2	3	4	5	6	7
Strongly						Strongly
Disagree						Agree

___ 1. I have told my friend that I love my spouse.

___ 2. My spouse and I have discussed our future together.

___ 3. I feel happier when I am with my spouse.

___ 4. Being together is very important to me.

___ 5. I cannot imagine a future with anyone other than my spouse.

___ 6. I feel that no one else can meet my needs as well as my spouse.

___ 7. When talking about my spouse and me, I tend to use the words.

"us", "we" and "our."

___ 8. I depend on my spouse to help me with many things in my life.

___ 9. I want to stay in this relationship no matter how hard times become in the future.

___10. I am willing to work on me so that I can be closer to my spouse.

Scoring: Add the numbers you assigned to each item. A 1 reflects the least involvement and a 7 reflects the most involvement. The lower your total score (10 is the lowest possible score), the lower your level of involvement; the higher your total score (70), the greater your level of involvement. A score of 40 places you at the midpoint between a very uninvolved and very involved relationship.

Letter to Abba:

Dear Abba Father,

God is not the author of confusion; He gives clarity and direction.

Father God, I ask for Your wisdom today. Help me slow my pace and attune my heart to Your voice. Thank You for loving me with an everlasting love and for forgiving me each time I call upon You. Teach me to extend that same forgiveness to others. Help me to show Your love even more deeply and consistently.

You are a God who leads and guides. Direct my steps in the path of righteousness in every area of my life, my personal reflection and time with You, my marriage, my family, my ministry, and my work. Grant me the wisdom of Solomon and the love of Jesus as I strengthen the spiritual muscles needed for a marriage that is whole, resilient, and lacking nothing.

I declare and decree that You have designed my marriage for success on every level. You have gone before me, preparing the way, so that my marriage reflects Christ's love for the church. For this, Heavenly Father, I am truly thankful.

In Jesus Name, Amen.

Continued Prayers,

Love Me

Go Deep

In 1966, the music group **The Temptations** released a song titled *"Beauty Is Only Skin Deep."* In one verse, they sing, *"My friends ask what do I see in you, but it goes deeper than the eye can view. You have a pleasing personality, and that's an ever-loving rare quality."* Their words echo a deeper truth: physical beauty fades with time and ultimately disappears in the grave (Ps. 49:14). It is temporary only "skin deep."

I once told my sons that we don't get to choose both ugly character and unattractive behavior; if we must choose, let us choose to be beautiful in character. After all, someone can be physically attractive and still be deeply unattractive in spirit. True beauty begins within, and it is this inner beauty that honors God and endures.

Have you ever paused to consider your own beauty?

Not the surface-level kind the world measures, but the beauty God Himself placed within you. We often find it easy to see beauty in others; our spouse, our children, our friends. Yet when it comes to seeing that same beauty in ourselves, the mirror can feel blurry.

Maybe you grew up hearing hurtful words, *too tall, too short, too big, too small,* or simply *not enough.* Those voices can linger long after childhood, echoing in moments when we're already feeling vulnerable. I can still remember some of the cruel things said to me, and how they made me question whether there was anything lovely about me at all.

But the truth of God cuts through every lie we've ever believed about ourselves.

God sees in ways we never could. He sees counterintuitively; beyond the surface, beyond our history, beyond the lies whispered over us. Every small seed of unworthiness the enemy planted early in our lives, God is faithful to uproot. And He replaces those lies with His truth:

"You are more than enough."

"He hath made everything beautiful in His time..." (Ecclesiastes 3:11)

The same God who shaped galaxies also shaped *you* with intention, care, and beauty. Even when we struggle to see it, He has already declared it. His workmanship in us is ongoing, unfolding day by day and part of our spiritual journey is learning to see ourselves through His eyes, not through the eyes of those who wounded us.

Take a moment today to breathe in this truth:

You are His creation.

You are His beauty. And in His perfect time, every part of your story is being made beautiful.

"Let the beauty of the Lord our God be upon us..." (Psalm 90:17)

Going into deeper places of the heart requires prayer. We must ask God to reveal His love to us, because He values what lies within our character and the qualities, He formed in us far more than outward charm or appearance. God told Samuel, **"People look at the outward appearance, but the Lord looks at the heart." (1 Samuel 16:7)**

As we grow, we learn that no personality is "better" than another. Each carries God-given strengths. When those strengths are left unrefined, they become weaknesses; but when surrendered to God, they become powerful tools for His work.

Maybe you're gifted at helping others. Maybe planning and organizing comes naturally.

Maybe you are a peacemaker who calms troubled hearts.

Own the strengths God has placed within you.

Use the "giftings" of your personality with confidence.

Acknowledge your weaknesses and invite the Lord to shape them.

Christ accepted Peter with both his strengths and his flaws just as He accepts us. When Jesus chose His disciples, He wasn't looking for perfection or outward impressiveness. He was looking for real people, people who could be transformed by His love, and then carry that love to others, even through failure. Yes people like you and I!

When you embrace your God-shaped personality, you will begin to discover the beautiful, powerful, and positive difference you can make in the lives of others. And you will see, perhaps more clearly than ever, the beauty God has already placed within you.

When you can see the beauty that God has placed in you, you can see the beauty that God has designed for your marriage.

Self- Compassion Test

Please read each statement carefully before answering. To the left of each statement indicate how often you behave in the stated manner, using the answer range below.

Answer Range: 1 - Almost Never

2 - Occasionally

3 - Sometimes

4 - Fairly Often

5 - Almost Always

____ I'm disapproving and judgmental about my own flaws and inadequacies.

_____When I'm feeling down, I tend to obsess and fixate on everything that's wrong.

--------- When I think about my inadequacies, it tends to make me feel more separate and cut off from the rest of the world.

_____ I try to be loving towards myself when I'm feeling emotional pain.

_____ I'm tolerant of my own flaws and inadequacies.

--------- I'm tolerant of others when they make a mistake.

------- When something upsets me, I get carried away with my feelings.

------ When something upsets me, I try to keep my emotions in balance.

Total Score	Self-Compassion Level Description
35 – 40	High Self-Compassion You respond to personal difficulty with kindness, balance, and emotional awareness.
34 – 28	Moderate Self-Compassion You show self-compassion in some areas but may still struggle with self-criticism or emotional overwhelm.
27 - 20	Low Self-Compassion You may be highly self-critical or feel isolated during challenges. Developing self-kindness and emotional balance could be helpful.
19 – Below-	Very Low Self-Compassion You likely experience strong self-judgment and emotional distress when facing difficulties. Support and intentional self-compassion practices are strongly recommended.

No matter how you answered, take time to find Scriptures that align your personality with

God's plan for your life. God desires not only that we show goodness and kindness to others but that we extend that same grace and kindness to ourselves.

Reflection:_____

_____

_____

_____

_____

_____

_____

_____

_____

_____

_____

_____

_____

_____

_____

Letter to Abba:

Dear Abba Father,

I thank You for leading me into the deep places with You. Thank You for creating me with beauty from the very depths of my being. Today, I surrender my thoughts to You so that I may continually put on the mind of Christ.

Help me to be kind, tenderhearted, and forgiving not only toward others, as You have been toward me, but also toward myself. Father, open my eyes to see myself the way You see me.

Thank You for destroying every attempt the enemy made to harm me and for restoring me through Your love. Thank You that I walk in complete healing mind, body, and spirit. Thank You for filling me afresh with Your Holy Spirit.

Thank You for my marriage. Thank You for teaching me how to love my spouse and how to build them up so that Your reflection shines through me. Thank You for bringing us together and making our union something beautiful in Your sight.

I am Your masterpiece, fashioned by Your hands, and for that I give You all the glory. In Jesus' Name I pray. Amen.

Continued Prayers,

Love Me

Running Tired

What happens when exhaustion settles into our lives? I remember a season when I was doing everything I could to keep my husband happy, care for our four sons, lead the PTSA, work a full-time job, serve in our church ministry, and pursue my doctorate. I was worn out; physically, emotionally, and spiritually. It felt as though there was no space left for myself, and even less time for *us* as a couple. I reached a point where I wondered how much longer I could keep going.

Have you ever felt like your soul desperately needed a recharge? When either you or your spouse becomes exhausted, the entire marriage can begin to feel drained. Arguments seem to surface more often, irritation rises quickly, and you may find yourselves becoming unpleasant without even realizing it. I can remember moments when I thought, *If I could just take a nap… if someone would just notice how tired I am.* Yet in the midst of my own weariness, I often forgot to pause and ask whether my husband was tired too!

There were moments when the guilt started to creep in as well. *How could I feel guilty for being tired?* I wondered. *Hasn't God called me to these responsibilities? Shouldn't I be relying on His strength? Am I being selfish? And how can I complain about exhaustion when others seem to carry even heavier loads with even greater pressure?*

Yet in those moments, I forgot the gentle invitation Jesus gives us in Matthew 11:28–29: *'Come unto me, all ye that labor and are heavy laden, and I will give you rest. Take my yoke upon you and learn of me; for I am meek and lowly in heart: and ye shall find rest unto your souls.'* His words remind us that our tiredness is not a sign of failure, it is a signal to draw closer to Him, to receive the rest only He can give.

I often wonder if people in the Bible wrestled with the same feelings of exhaustion that we do. The disciples certainly had to, thinking on Jesus' ministry and busy schedule, teaching the masses, healing the sick, deliverance, serving crowds that constantly pressed in on them, and offering continual care to those in need. Jesus' response to their weariness was full of compassion: *Because so many people were coming and going that they did not even have a chance to eat, he said to them, "Come with me by yourselves to a quiet place and get some rest"'* (Mark 6:31). Even in the midst of great ministry, Jesus recognized their need for rest and invited them into it.

Rest is not a weakness, it's a weapon. It restores what life drains from us. When we pause, our minds become clearer, our bodies begin to heal, and our spirits find room to breathe again. Just as a device needs to be plugged in when its battery runs low, we too must plug into Jesus.

In His presence, we find the strength to be "charged" back to full. It is as though He gently whispers, *"Come away and abide with Me, and you will find rest."*

God, the One who formed our minds, bodies, and souls knows our limitations better than we do. And He doesn't just understand them from a distance. Jesus, the Son of God, walked this earth and experienced the full weight of physical, emotional, and mental exhaustion. There were moments when He told His disciples to step away and rest, even though the needs around them were still great. Rest was not optional; it was sacred.

So how do we care well for ourselves and for those God has entrusted to us?

Consider Elijah. After a mighty victory on Mount Carmel, he found himself depleted, afraid, and ready to give up as he fled from Jezebel. Elijah, one of Scripture's greatest prophets hit his breaking point. And how did

God respond? Not with rebuke, but with compassion. God provided exactly what Elijah needed: rest, water, and bread (1 Kings 19:4–8). Sometimes the most spiritual thing we can do is simply sleep, eat, and allow God to refresh our weary souls.

There are certainly times when our exhaustion has deeper roots. Yet often, the first step toward healing is recognizing that we simply need to rest and that God Himself invites us to do so. *"I will refresh the weary and satisfy the faint"* (Jeremiah 31:25).

In marriage, it's easy to overlook the simple truth that sometimes our spouse is just tired and that's okay. What matters is that we remain attentive. We are called to check in with one another, to ask how the other is truly feeling, and to lean in wherever we can to ease the pressure. Often the greatest gift we can give our spouse is a gentle reminder to slow down, rest, and "plug into" Jesus for the recharge their heart needs.

When we consider the life of Jesus, we see that He modeled servant leadership in everything He did. And our servanthood begins not in public ministry, but at home. Serving our spouse is not a burden; it is a blessing and an honor. When we intentionally serve our marriage with love, humility, and grace, we will find that our marriage begins to serve us as well; strengthening, uplifting, and refreshing us in return.

Reflection:_____

_____

_____

_____

_____

_____

_____

_____

_____

_____

_____

_____

_____

_____

Letter to Abba:

Dear Abba Father,

Thank You for the strength You give me whenI am weary. Lord, You see the moments when I feel overwhelmed by my schedule, my responsibilities, and the weight of daily life.

Grant me wisdom to know when to rest and the grace to receive the rest You lovingly provide. Fill me with Your strength and stamina so I may faithfully fulfill the calling You have placed on my life.

Father, I lift up my spouse to You as well. Strengthen them for every assignment You have given and surround them with Your protection. Let each responsibility not drain them but instead become fuel for the journey You have prepared for them.

Abba, thank You for loving me even in my weakness and for blessing me with peaceful, restorative sleep. I ask that You extend that same sweet rest to my entire family. I love You, Lord, and I thank You for Your constant care, compassion, and presence. In Jesus Name! Amen.

Continued Prayers,

Love Me

A Momma's Prayer

There are some things you simply cannot understand… until God allows you to understand!

When my husband and I got married at twenty-one, we barely knew anything about life. All we really knew was that we loved each other and believed God had brought us together, no matter what anyone else thought. And let me tell you, the first half of our marriage was anything but easy. We stumbled, we struggled, and we had seasons where we wondered if we would ever find our footing.

But even in the middle of our mess, God was weaving something beautiful. He blessed our union with four incredible sons and a whole family of "bonus children" we never expected. At the time, we couldn't understand why God kept sending people into our lives who needed guidance, encouragement, or a place to land…

especially when *we* felt like the ones who needed help.

Have you ever been there? Have you ever asked God, "Why are You sending me people to pour into when I feel empty myself?"

What I've learned is this: sometimes God trusts us with others not because we are strong, but because He is shaping something strong *within us*. Sometimes He lets us minister while we're still mending. And sometimes the very people we think we are helping become part of our healing.

God doesn't wait for us to have it all together before He uses us. He uses us so that, through serving, loving, and showing up for others, *we* begin to understand what He has been doing in our own hearts all along.

I still remember holding our first son in my arms, staring into those tiny eyes and thinking, *Lord, what a precious gift You've given me.* In that moment, all I wanted was to shield him from every kind of hurt or pain. I wanted his world to be safe, gentle, and full of joy. And when God blessed us with three more sons, those same protective prayers filled my heart again.

God had already given a word for how I was feeling…."Children are a heritage from the Lord, offspring a reward from him. Like arrows in the hands of a warrior are children born in one's youth (Psalm 127:3)."

As their mother, I longed for them never to face rejection, fear, or disappointment. I wanted to be the barrier between them and anything that could wound them. But as they grew, I quickly learned there were some things I simply could not protect them from. The world is imperfect… and so am I.

I can still remember how something as small as them having a runny nose or a hurtful comment from a friend would break *my* heart. Their pain felt like my own. And each time I found myself crushed that I couldn't shield them from everything, God gently reminded me:

"You were never meant to be their Savior. You were called to be their mother."

There is a holy surrender in parenting, an understanding that the One who gave us these precious lives loves them even more than we do. And while we can guide, nurture, and pray over them, only God can protect their hearts in ways we cannot reach.

He teaches us to trust Him not just with our own lives… but with the lives we love most.

The Gift of Praying Forward

Just when I thought motherhood was only about protecting and providing, God gave me an unexpected hope; He taught me how to pray for my children. It was as if He whispered, *"You may not be able to shield them from everything, but you can cover them in prayer."*

So, I began praying intentionally over the lives of my four sons. I prayed that God would bless each one with a wife who would love Him first and love them deeply. I prayed that their lives would overflow with the kind of joy only the Lord can give; a joy rooted in the understanding that walking with God is the greatest success they could ever know.

And then God showed me something even more beautiful: praying for my children is itself a gift. The ability to lift their names before the throne of grace is evidence of His covenant love. I realized I could pray not only for my sons, but for my grandchildren and great-grandchildren; generations I may never meet, yet God already knows. I could even include my bonus babies in the prayer and God would honor my prayers because He filled me with His love. The kind of love that covered children that He gave me spiritually.

And God didn't stop there

He reminded me that His love in me was big enough, wide enough, and strong enough to cover not only my four sons, but also my *bonus babies*—the children He entrusted to me spiritually. So, I began to include them in my prayers as well, believing that God would honor those prayers because He was the One who placed that love in my heart.

It was His love that allowed me to embrace children who didn't come from my body but came straight from His heart. And because He gave them to me spiritually, I could lift them up spiritually confident that He hears and responds to every prayer born out of His love within me.

Because He is a covenant-keeping God, my prayers can reach further than my lifetime ever will.

Part of that covenant blessing is teaching our children what a relationship with God truly looks like. Not perfection, but devotion. Not flawless living, but faithful walking. As our sons watched my husband and me follow the Lord, they didn't see perfect parents; they saw parents who belonged to a perfect Father. They saw repentance, growth, grace, and the steady hand of God guiding us.

And in that, they learned the most important truth:

It is not our perfection that shapes the next generation, but our pattern of returning to the One who is perfect ….Abba Father. For this I am beyond grateful!

Reflection:_____

Write your own Prayer for your Children
(Be Intentional in your prayer):

_____

_____

_____

_____

_____

_____

_____

_____

_____

_____

_____

_____

_____

_____

_____

_____

_____

_____

_____

_____

_____

_____

_____

_____

_____

_____

_____

_____

Letter to Abba:

Dear Abba Father,

Thank You for entrusting me with the precious gift of my family. Thank You that when I fall short, You are faithful to pick up the pieces and continue Your work in us. I am grateful for every beautiful trait You have placed within each one of them.

Lord, if there is anything in their hearts, or in mine that does not please You, gently reveal it so we may grow into the people You desire us to be. Thank You for the generations I have not yet met, and for the promise that they will come from a lineage of people who walked by faith and sought to honor You with their whole lives.

Father, let my children and grandchildren hear Your voice clearly and never follow a stranger. Remind them daily that they can bring every hurt, every fear, and every disappointment to You, because You care for them more deeply than we ever could.

Give them forgiving hearts and a desire to pursue Your kingdom above all else. Promote and establish them in every area of their lives according to Your will so that their victories become testimonies that bring You glory.

Bless their spouses, Lord, and draw them together in unity, love, and purpose as they become one in You.

In Jesus' mighty name, **Amen.**

Continued Prayers,

Love Me

A Fathers Strength

Fathers are a gift from God, His strong hand in the family structure. God designed them to work, to provide, and to carry the weight of responsibility with quiet courage. Day after day they labor so their families can have what they need, often without applause or recognition. This is part of the divine calling placed within them: to reflect God's steady provision.

Yet beneath that strength lies a tenderness that can be easy to overlook. A father's love often shows up in action more than words, in long hours rather than long speeches. If we are not careful, we may miss the sensitive heart behind the hard work, the desire every father carries for his family to feel cherished, supported, and secure.

Many fathers also bear the burden of discipline, guiding their children with firm hands and steady boundaries so they can grow into responsible adults who bless their communities. In this role, they are sometimes misunderstood; sternness mistaken for harshness, fatigue mistaken for indifference. But behind it all is a love that corrects, protects, and gently points toward wisdom.

Today, let us pause to give thanks for the fathers God has placed in our lives. Let us look not only at what they do, but at the heart behind it: a heart designed by the Father above.

Silent Lessons….

I often find myself quietly watching my husband as he interacts with our sons. Sometimes they're working under the hood of a car, sometimes building a table, and sometimes just talking in the breeze. And in those simple moments, I see something sacred; the very things he prayed for early in our marriage, God has graciously granted. I see the spark in his eyes, the pride in his smile, the joy of a father whose prayers have been answered in the form of four strong sons.

Only I know the depth of the journey that brought him here. The trauma he endured as a young boy; growing up below the poverty level, caring for an ailing mother, with no father and little family support. I remember the fear he carried at the thought of becoming a dad, afraid he didn't have enough to give. He used to pray that God would simply send someone along to bless him with what he lacked.

But God had a different plan. Instead of giving him someone to depend on, God entrusted him with four leaders to raise; four young men who would carry strength, character, and purpose.

There are moments when I see him searching for words to share his past, to explain why he responds the way he does. But he also knows that some lessons can't be spoken. Some truths his sons won't fully understand until life places them in the same position he once stood.

It isn't easy for him. A father longs to shield his children from pain, to help them avoid the heartaches he endured. Yet he recognizes that some struggles are shaping tools in God's hands, forming boys into men, men into leaders. Every challenge, every disappointment, every hard-earned lesson carries the potential to grow them into the wise, steady men God is molding them to be.

So, he practices patience. He gives guidance where he can and offers silence where God needs to teach. And in that quiet restraint, I see a deeper love, the kind that trusts God to complete the work He has begun in their lives. We safeguard so many areas of our lives that it becomes second nature, and before we realize it, those habits can keep us from seeing the true condition of our hearts.

In marriage, we can easily take for granted the experiences that formed our spouses into who they are today. But God uses every event, both theirs and ours, to shape our hearts and ultimately bring glory to His name.

Every father carries hopes and expectations for his children dreams about what they might become, where life may take them, or even whom they might one day marry. Some may wonder whether it's normal for parents to live vicariously through their children. I'm not sure the answer is simple, but this much I do know:

wanting your children to excel, to experience more, and to live a better life than you did is a natural and loving desire.

His Hopes....

It's not always easy being a father. Many men never had a dad who modeled fatherhood well, and some have never met their fathers at all. Yet God, in His wisdom, still calls them to step into a role they may have never seen lived out before.

Fatherhood is deeply fulfilling, exhilarating at times, overflowing with joy and pride. But it can also be frustrating, painful, and exhausting. There are moments when a father longs to fix what's broken in his child's life but discovers that he can't. Times when the answers simply aren't there, and all he feels is the weight of helplessness. "As a father has compassion on his children, so the Lord has compassion on those who fear him" (Psalm 103:13).

God has compassion so it's in those very moments that God reminds earthly fathers of something powerful: they were never meant to carry the role alone. God is the perfect Father who fills in every gap, strengthens every weakness, and guides every man who turns to Him. When fathers reach the end of themselves, God steps in with wisdom, peace, and grace that cannot be mustered on human strength alone.

The challenges of fatherhood don't expose a man's failures they reveal his need for God. And that dependence is exactly where God does His greatest work.

There is a deep joy that fills a father's heart when he sees his children thriving. When a child succeeds, whether at a young age or later in life, a father feels a sense of mission accomplished, like his love, guidance, and prayers have taken root.

Watching a child's marriage flourish, seeing them earn a promotion, start a business, or welcome their own children into the world; all of it becomes a beautiful reminder that God's plan is unfolding in His perfect timing. A father plants seeds, but it is God who brings the growth. And in every milestone, every achievement, every answered prayer, God is quietly revealing His faithfulness through the generations.

Reflection:_____

_____

_____

_____

_____

_____

_____

_____

_____

_____

_____

_____

_____

_____

_____

_____

_____

_____

Letter to Abba:

Dear Abba Father,

Thank You for the gift of fathers, imperfect yet deeply valuable, strong yet tender. Help us recognize the love behind their labor and the purpose behind their discipline. Strengthen every father today, fill them with renewed grace, and remind them that You see every sacrifice, even when others do not. May Your presence encourage them as they lead their families.

Lord, open our eyes to the delicate, intricate details You weave into our lives, those small things we often overlook yet make us into the beautiful souls You designed us to be. Give us patience when impatience rises within us and grant us peace in every circumstance. Teach us to speak love freely and to express appreciation generously.

Keep at the forefront of our minds that we are created in Your marvelous image, and that everything You have made, You declared good. Abba Father, we love You and thank You. In Jesus' Name, Amen.

Continued Prayers,

Love Me

Love View

Marriage begins for many different reasons some practical, some personal, but the reason most commonly named, and most deeply longed for, is LOVE. In 1994, actor Jamie Foxx released a song titled *Infatuation*. It was one of my favorite songs at the time. In the lyrics, he wrestles with an honest question: does the woman he loves truly love him in return, or is what she feels merely infatuation? That question lingers because it reflects a challenge many couples face, even within marriage learning to distinguish between fleeting feelings and lasting covenant love.

Infatuation is often mistaken for love, especially in the early stages of a relationship. Yet Scripture reminds us that not everything that feels good is good or lasting. The word *infatuation* is rooted in foolishness, and the

Bible warns us that emotions without wisdom can lead us astray. *"There is a way that seems right to a man, but its end is the way of death"* (Proverbs 14:12). Infatuation thrives on passion and attraction, but it lacks the foundation necessary to sustain a marriage commitment, truth, and endurance. It may ignite quickly, but it cannot carry a couple through trials.

True marital love looks very different from the world's definition of romance. It is not sustained by constant excitement or emotional heights. Instead, it deepens over time and is marked by patience, faithfulness, sacrifice, and security. Scripture defines this love clearly: *"Love is patient, love is kind… It bears all things, believes all things, hopes all things, endures all things"* (1 Corinthians 13:4, 7). This kind of love is not driven by feeling, but by daily choice a choice to forgive, to remain, and to serve one another. Marriage reflects the heart of God's covenant love. Just as husbands and wives are called to remain faithful through every season, God's love toward us is steadfast and unchanging. *"The steadfast love of the Lord never ceases; His mercies never come to an end"* (Lamentations 3:22). As married couples grow in understanding the difference between infatuation and true love, they are invited to love one another not with shallow passion, but with faithful devotion a love that endures, matures, and glorifies God through every season of marriage.

Conditions for Love

As a young girl, I remember playing outside with my friends, talking about love, playing house, and cradling our baby dolls as if they were our own children. Much of what we acted out was simply a reflection of what we had observed in our own homes; imitating the rhythms, roles, and relationships of our mothers and fathers. Even then, our understanding of love was being quietly formed.

Alongside those experiences were the fairy tales' stories of Cinderella, Snow White, and happily-ever-after endings. These stories shaped our early expectations, teaching us to believe that love was effortless, magical, and always triumphant. Without realizing it, many of us carried those childhood images of love into adulthood and eventually into marriage.

Yet marriage reveals that love is not a fairy tale, but a daily choice. It is learned, practiced, and refined through real life through patience, forgiveness, and perseverance. Scripture reminds us, *"When I was a child, I spoke like a child… when I became an adult, I put an end to childish ways"* (1 Corinthians 13:11).

The same is true for young boys, many of them once saw girls as "gross," until the day curiosity turned into care. As married couples, we are invited to grow beyond imagined ideals and embrace a deeper, truer love one that reflects Christ's faithful love for His people.

Love is often described as a feeling something we fall into and hope to hold onto. Our society reinforces this idea daily through music, movies, television, and novels. These messages tell us that love is an experience to be chased, enjoyed, and measured by emotion, and that if we are not "in love," we are somehow missing out. Over time, this way of thinking can quietly shape how husbands and wives evaluate their marriages.

Yet feelings are fragile. They rise and fall with circumstances, stress, and seasons of life. Scripture reminds us that love was never meant to rest on emotion alone. In marriage, love is not merely something we feel it is something we choose. *"Above all, love each other deeply, because love covers over a multitude of sins"* (1 Peter 4:8). Deep love is not passive; it is intentional and enduring.

In contrast to modern culture, more traditional societies have understood marriage differently. In places where marriages are arranged, romantic love is not the starting point but the result of commitment. While these practices differ from biblical marriage, they remind us of an important truth: lasting love grows where faithfulness, responsibility, and shared purpose are present. Scripture affirms this principle when it says, *"Two are better than one… If either of them falls down, one can help the other up"* (Ecclesiastes 4:9–10).

Biblical marriage is neither driven solely by emotion nor controlled by culture. It is a covenant before God. Husbands and wives are called to love one another sacrificially, not conditionally. *"Husbands, love your wives, just as Christ loved the church and gave Himself up for her"* (Ephesians 5:25). This kind of love does not wait for perfect feelings it acts in obedience and trust.

When couples stop chasing the idea of love as an emotion and begin practicing love as a commitment, marriages are strengthened. Love becomes less about what we receive and more about what we give. In this way, marriage reflects God's faithful love steady, purposeful, and unchanging.

Reflection:_____

_____

_____

_____

_____

_____

_____

_____

_____

_____

_____

_____

_____

_____

_____

_____

_____

Letter to Abba:

Dear Abba Father,

Lord, thank You that we have the mind of Christ. Help us not to romanticize or elevate our emotions above Your truth, but to anchor our marriage in commitment, humility, and service. Teach us to love one another not only with our feelings, but with faithful actions that honor You.

May we see the love within our marriage as a reflection of Your love; steady, selfless, and enduring. In every season, let our union bring glory to Your name. In areas where we are weak, help us to lean fully into You, trusting Your strength to sustain us.

Let our marriage be a living testimony to other couples who are seeking You. May they see in us a reflection of Your grace, faithfulness, and covenant love. Help us to walk worthy of the calling You have placed upon our lives and upon our marriage.

Draw us into deeper communion with You than we have ever known. Teach us to walk in complete surrender, so that we may serve one another as You have called us to; demonstrating our full trust in You in every area of our lives.

Amen.

Continued Prayers,

Love Me

Angels Touch

If I asked you what brings you comfort, would you know?

Life has thrown many curveballs my way; some with lessons I clearly understand, others that I still wrestle with, wondering why they happened. I suspect most of us can relate to that feeling of uncertainty.

One afternoon, I went to pick up my eldest son from school early for a physical. As I waited in the hallway, my eyes fell on a poem on the wall, written by a second grader. It was titled *"At Night I Touch an Angel's Face."*

I was immediately intrigued. In the poem, the child described how, after his parents read the Bible to him, an angel would come into his room, not white, not black, but simply an angel of a bronze shade. This angel would lean down over his bed, and the child would touch its face before drifting off to sleep.

As I reached the end of the poem, my heart stopped. I realized that my son had written it. Stunned, I got into the car with him, hesitating to ask if he had made it up, but deep down, I already knew he hadn't. When I finally asked, he confirmed it was all true.

In that moment, I felt comforted, and I was reminded of something powerful: God often shows His presence in ways we do not expect, and His reassurance can come through the smallest, most ordinary moments.

I wondered what else my son saw or experienced, and why I hadn't noticed some of the same things. Was I too busy? Had I not been paying attention? Or was this God's gentle way of getting my attention?

Some things are not for us to fully understand. Yet one thing was clear: my son was not afraid. He was delighted to share the experience of the angel who entered his room, as if he wanted me to see what he saw.

It was in that moment that God began to speak to me about having a *childlike faith*. Jesus Himself calls us to this kind of trust: *"Truly I tell you, unless you change and become like little children, you will never enter the kingdom of heaven"* (Matthew 18:3). God was inviting me to trust Him in every area of my life not just in the extraordinary moments, but in the ordinary and unseen.

The Bible also reminds us: *"Trust in the Lord with all your heart and lean not on your own understanding; in all your ways submit to Him, and He will make your paths straight"* (Proverbs 3:5–6). Like a child, we are called to look to Him with wonder, to believe even when we cannot fully comprehend, and to rejoice in His presence.

Maybe that was it…. even my son seemed to sense that this experience brought him a deep sense of peace and comfort. This was not the kind of comfort we feel from familiar pleasures, like being at Grandma's house on

Christmas. Nope….this was a profound, soul deep comfort, a reassurance that there is no lack, no worry and no need for concern.

It reminded me that God desires to give His children this same complete comfort. *"He makes me lie down in green pastures, He leads me beside the still waters, He restores my soul"* (Psalm 23:2-3).

Sometimes we take children for granted or we make statements such as, "He/she is just a child they don't know!"

Children are a heritage of the Lord, pay attention because God will use them to get your attention or to remind you to keep the child like faith you once walked in.

Even in the chaos of life God calls us to pause, to listen to His voice, and to enter the place of rest and peace that only He can provide.

This is the type of truth that is important in marriage. Life together will be unpredictable and sometimes overwhelming, but when we seek God together, when we pause and follow His guidance, His peace can settle over our hearts and our homes. This kind of comfort strengthens our marriage, reminding us that our ultimate security is found not in circumstances, but in the loving presence of

As married couples, life will throw its curveballs at us too, stress, misunderstandings, or seasons of uncertainty. But just as I found comfort in seeing God's touch in my child's life, we can find His presence in our marriage. Through prayer, Scripture, acts of love, and even small moments of connection, God reminds us that we are never alone. He is there, leaning over our hearts, giving us strength, peace, and hope for each day.

Let us choose to notice these moments together, to see His fingerprints in our marriage, and to let His comfort guide how we love and serve one another.

Reflection:_____

_____

_____

_____

_____

_____

_____

_____

_____

_____

_____

_____

_____

_____

_____

_____

_____

_____

_____

Letter to Abba:

Dear Abba Father,

Thank You for Your presence in our lives, even in the quiet, ordinary moments. Help us, as a couple, to notice Your gentle touch and the ways You speak to us, sometimes in ways we cannot fully understand.

Teach us to approach our marriage with childlike faith, trusting You together in every joy and every challenge. Just as a child delights in Your angels and Your protection, let us delight in Your guidance, resting in the assurance that You are always near.

Lord, help us to see Your fingerprints in our home, in our conversations, in our acts of love. May we recognize Your comfort when life feels uncertain, and may we draw strength from knowing You are leaning over our hearts, giving us peace, hope, and courage.

Fill our marriage with wonder and trust, that we may honor You in how we love, serve, and care for one another. Let our hearts be a place where Your presence dwells, bringing rest, joy, and the assurance that we are never alone.

In Jesus' name, Amen.

Continued Prayers,

Love Me

Establishing Value

I remember April of 2018, when a friend invited me to hear Benjamin Watson speak at the Forum in Rome, GA. Benjamin had written a blog about racial tension that turned into a book titled *Under Our Skin.* Before attending this event, my friend (the one who invited me) and I had spent several weeks meeting at a local coffee shop and sharing our stories. Our intention was to have honest conversations about the hard subjects in life.

We came from different backgrounds and held slightly different beliefs, yet we shared a deep love for Jesus, a love for people, and many of the same core values. Despite our differences, God guided us in learning how to truly understand one another. He showed us how to listen with empathy and grace, even when our perspectives were shaped by very different experiences.

Through these conversations, I was reminded of Proverbs 27:17:

"As iron sharpens iron, so one person sharpens another." God uses relationships even those that challenge us to refine our hearts, expand our understanding, and teach us patience, humility, and love. When we engage with others openly and respectfully, we allow Him to bridge gaps that our own understanding could never span. She had been married for about the same length of time as I had. Like me, she had children, each with their own unique challenges. Even our parents influenced the paths we were on, shaping the ways we approached life, relationships, and family. Nevertheless, we always had good conversations, we prayed for each other and blessed God for allowing our paths to cross.

Meeting Benjamin Watson was inspiring; he was a humble Christian man, passionate about bridging gaps and helping people see each other through God's eyes. Which is exactly what me and my friend had done…we had begun to bridge some gaps.

Watson talked about things that people tried to stay clear of…. such as remembering the first time you noticed you were different from your friends.

His message stayed with me, because it reminded me of a truth, we all wrestle with at some point: our sense of identity. Have you ever felt like you were "not enough" perhaps because of your skin color, your hair, your background, or the way you look? Maybe you've compared yourself to others and felt like you didn't measure up.

The Bible reminds us that our worth and Identity are not defined by what others think or by societal standards. God says: *"So God created mankind in his own image, in the image of God he created them; male and female he created them"* (Genesis 1:27).

You are intentionally and beautifully made, just as you are. Your hair, your skin, your talents, your quirks; they are all part of God's design. The psalmist echoes this truth when he declares:

"I praise you because I am fearfully and wonderfully made; your works are wonderful, I know that full well" (Psalm 139:14).

Even when the world tells us otherwise, we can remember that our identity is secure in Christ:

"Therefore, if anyone is in Christ, the new creation has come: The old has gone, the new is here!" (2 Corinthians 5:17).

Knowing this transforms how we see ourselves and how we relate to others. It gives us confidence to celebrate our uniqueness and to honor others as God's creations too. It also calls us to humility, love, and unity just like Benjamin Watson encourages in his work, bridging divides and fostering understanding.

Today, let's choose to anchor our identity in God, not in fleeting human standards. Let's embrace the beauty He has placed in us and around us, seeing ourselves and others as He sees us: beloved, valuable, and wonderfully made.

- What messages have you believed about yourself that are not from God?
- How can you remind yourself daily that your identity is secure in Him?

Remember to think of yourself as valuable! God said everything that He made was good. You are so valuable that Christ died and rose for you! There is nothing more valuable than that!

Reflection:_____

Letter to Abba:

Dear Abba Father,

Thank You for creating me in Your image, fearfully and wonderfully made (Psalm 139:14). I confess that too often I compare myself to others, wishing I looked or acted differently, forgetting that You have uniquely crafted every detail of me.

Lord, help me to embrace the skin You gave me, not with pride, but with gratitude and peace. Teach me to see myself through Your eyes, to recognize that my worth is not measured by appearances, achievements, or the approval of others, but by Your unfailing love. Remind me that Your purpose for my life is greater than my insecurities, and that every part of me, inside and out, has meaning and value in Your kingdom. Help me walk in confidence, not arrogance, celebrating the beauty of the body, mind, and spirit You have entrusted to me.

Give me courage to care for myself with respect, kindness, and joy, knowing that honoring the life You gave me glorifies You. May I also extend that same grace to others, seeing them as You see them: precious, unique, and beloved.

Lord, let me rest in the truth that I am enough because You are enough. Teach me to trust that Your plan for me, just as I am, is perfect. Fill me with peace in the skin You have given me and let Your light shine through me each day.

In Jesus' name, Amen.

Continued Prayers,

Love Me

Walking Together

In Amos 3:3–8, the prophet invites us to pause and consider a series of searching questions. *Can two walk together unless they are in agreement?* Just as a lion does not roar without cause, and a bird does not fall into a snare without a trap being set, Amos reminds us that nothing happens apart from purpose and intention.

These images call us to examine our own walk with God. Are we moving in step with Him, aligned with His will and His ways? God's voice, like the roar of a lion, is never empty or meaningless. When He speaks, it is because something is unfolding, an invitation to listen, to respond, and to trust.

This passage encourages us to reflect on our relationship with the Lord. Agreement with God is not merely belief, but obedience and attentiveness. As we walk in harmony with Him, we grow more aware of His guidance and more responsive to His call.

We all possess a measure of faith, even if we don't fully understand how to measure it or what it truly means. Romans 12:3 reminds us: *"For by the grace given to me, I say to everyone among you not to think of himself more highly than he ought to think, but to think with sober judgment, each according to the measure of faith that God has assigned."*

There was a season in our marriage when I had no real understanding of what it meant to be "on one accord." All I knew was that he was always calling the shots, and I felt I was simply supposed to follow. From his perspective, all he knew was that he was supposed to lead, and I was supposed to follow.

No one had taken the time to guide us in setting healthy boundaries or teaching us how to grow together as a team. More importantly, how to walk together in agreement. We were navigating marriage without a clear understanding of unity, balance, and shared purpose.

For many of us, traditional teaching emphasized a single perspective: *"The man is the head of the household."* While leadership in a marriage is important, there was often little explanation of what it truly meant to be a helpmate. Newlyweds were left to navigate their roles without guidance on partnership, mutual respect, or shared purpose.

God's Word offers a clearer picture of marriage as a partnership built on love, respect, and unity. Genesis 2:18 reminds us: *"The Lord God said, 'It is not good for the man to be alone. I will make a helper suitable for him.'"* Being a helper doesn't mean being lesser it means walking alongside, complementing one another, and sharing life together in love. Ephesians 5:21 adds:

"Submit to one another out of reverence for Christ."

In marriage, we are not called to dominate or demand, but to walk together in humility. It is not about one leading by force and the other complying, but about two hearts seeking God's will as one. Marriage is not a one-sided arrangement; it is a call to mutual submission, respect, and care, reflecting God's love in the relationship.

As couples, we can grow together by learning to communicate, honor each other's perspectives, and build a marriage that reflects God's design. True partnership comes when both spouses understand their value, roles, and purpose in the marriage, working as a team rather than following rigid expectations.

Questions to Ponder:

- In what areas of your marriage could you grow in mutual partnership and understanding?

- How can you honor your spouse as a true helper and equal in God's eyes?

As couples, it's easy to struggle with uncertainty. We may wonder if we're walking in God's plan for our lives, if we truly hear His voice, or even if we're praying "correctly." The questions can feel endless. But faith is not about having all the answers it's about trusting God together, even when the path is unclear.

The opposite of faith is sight. The world teaches us to see first and then believe, but Scripture calls us to believe first, trusting that God will fulfill His promises. Together, as husband and wife, you can encourage one another to step forward in faith, to lean on God's guidance, and to remind each other that His timing is perfect.

When uncertainty comes, and it will, hold onto each other and onto God. Pray together, listen together, and step forward together in the faith He has given each of you. Over time, you'll see His promises unfold, and your shared faith will strengthen not only your individual walk with God but also your marriage.

Questions to Ponder:

- How can you encourage your spouse to walk in faith when uncertainty arises?
- What step of faith is God calling you to take together as a couple?

These are the thoughts that should occupy our minds!

Reflection:_____

_____

_____

_____

_____

_____

_____

_____

_____

_____

_____

_____

_____

—————————————————

—————————————————

—————————————————

—————————————————

—————————————————

—————————————————

Letter to Abba:

Dear Abba Father,

Lord, we place our lives and our marriage fully in Your hands. Strengthen the measure of faith You have planted within each of us and teach us to encourage one another as we walk faithfully with You. Help us to believe before we see, trusting that You are always faithful to fulfill every promise You have spoken.

Form within us a bond that is unbreakable rooted first in You and strengthened through our love for one another. Grant us unmeasured strength and wisdom as we build the ministry

You have called us to steward and serve the people You have entrusted to us.

When we lack answers or cannot see the outcome, remind us that it is enough to simply come and sit at Your feet. We surrender every intimate detail of our lives to You, trusting in Your perfect will and unfailing love.

In Jesus' name, Amen.

Continued Prayers,

Love Me

The Home

My grandmother often said, "If these walls could talk, oh the story they would tell." Depending on the age of the home, I can only image the lessons, and stories that have echoed through the rooms over the years. Each wall holds whispers of the past, reminders of love, perseverance and faith that have shaped the lives of those who lived there. Much like the good stories those walls also hold the traumas and whispers of fear.

Regardless of the stories that echo through the walls, each marriage carries its own trials and opportunities for growth, shaping the hearts of those who walk within it. Many enter marriage carrying a beautiful picture in their hearts; a house on a hill with a white picket fence, filled effortlessly with friendship, intimacy, laughter, and abundance. In this vision, the children are well-behaved and thriving, resources are plentiful, and even the smallest details fall neatly into place. It is an appealing dream, and one many of us hold as we say, *"I do."*

Yet marriage is not a ready-made house waiting to be occupied. It is a foundation God invites two people to build together. Love does not automatically reside in the institution of marriage; it lives in the hearts of the husband and wife who choose, day by day, to pour it in. Romance is not something we inherit, it is something we cultivate through intention, patience, and sacrifice.

The house on the hill is not an illusion because it is impossible, but because it is unfinished. Every room must be built. Every wall must be strengthened. Everything that fills that home will be there because you labored together, prayed together, forgave often, and trusted God through the process.

Yes, the dream can become real, but it requires work, grace, and perseverance. When a marriage is built on faith, commitment, and love poured out daily, God is faithful to turn effort into beauty and partnership into a home worth standing in.

Foundation....

Couples who learn to build a dream together often reap the benefits of a beautiful home. I have often shared this truth in quiet conversations with my husband. People frequently comment on how beautiful our home is when they visit. And I am grateful for that. Yet the true beauty of a home is not found in the furniture, the décor, or the rug at the front door. It is found in the love within it.

The foundation of our home and everything placed in it has been built intentionally, through patience, forgiveness, prayer, and mutual respect. It is the love that greets people when they walk in the door: the kind of love that makes children linger a little longer and allows adults to feel safe enough to remove their shoes, rest, and breathe.

Scripture reminds us that the heart of a home begins with the people who dwell within it:

- *"Above all, love each other deeply, because love covers over a multitude of sins"* (1 Peter 4:8).

- *"By wisdom a house is built, and through understanding it is established; through knowledge its rooms are filled with rare and beautiful treasures"* (Proverbs 24:3–4).

- *"Do everything in love"* (1 Corinthians 16:14).

A Christ-centered marriage creates a home that is more than just walls and furniture. It becomes a place of refuge, a sanctuary of peace, and a living testimony of God's love. As husbands and wives, when we choose to love intentionally, to serve one another, and to welcome others in kindness, we build a home that reflects God's heart.

Windows & Doors….

When I was younger, my grandmother had a strict routine: every evening, she would lock all the doors and secure the windows. She had so many locks and chains that even someone with a key could not get in once the hour passed. She would also place wood between the windowpanes and latches, ensuring nothing unwanted could enter her home. If you were not inside before curfew, the front porch was your bedroom unless prior arrangements had been made.

Windows and doors are essential to a home, they protect it, define its boundaries, and determine what comes in and what stays out. Similarly, in marriage, what we allow into our hearts, our minds, and our relationship profoundly impacts the foundation of our home.

When we build a home, we ensure the windows and doors are insulated, air-tight, and positioned to let in light but keep out harm. We

even install alarms to guard against intruders.
Marriage requires the same intentional care:

- Guard your doors, the entrances of your marriage, like trust, communication, and intimacy. Protect them from negativity, betrayal, and distractions.

- Secure your windows, the places that let in influences from the outside world. Ensure they allow in light, wisdom, and encouragement, but block out what can weaken or harm your bond.

- Set boundaries, just as my grandmother enforced a curfew, establish boundaries that protect your marriage and your family.

Scripture reminds us in Proverbs 4:23: "Above all else, guard your heart, for everything you do flows from it." Just as a well-secured home is safe and welcoming, a marriage protected with love, trust, and discernment will flourish.

Take a moment today to examine the doors and windows of your marriage. What needs to be secured? What should you allow in to bring light and growth? Guard your home, guard your heart, and watch your marriage thrive.

Reflection:_____

_____

_____

_____

_____

_____

_____

_____

_____

_____

_____

_____

_____

_____

_____

_____

_____

_____

Letter to Abba:

Dear Abba Father,

Thank You for building a strong foundation of Your Word in my heart. Thank You that my home is blessed and secured by Your angels of light, and that the walls of my heart echo Your love, kindness, and grace.

Lord, help me to continue building upon the firm foundation You have laid before me. Give me wisdom in every area of my life, my finances, my investments, and in the people, I allow into my home. Help me to manage my time wisely, always seeking understanding and knowledge, and to make choices that honor You.

Thank You, Father, for going before me and preparing the way. Thank You for granting me favor with those I must work with, and for guiding me in opportunities to serve and lead with integrity. I am grateful that You allow me to teach others how to steward their spiritual lives, families, time, and resources with discernment and love.

May my life, my home, and all that I do reflect Your goodness. May I always walk in Your wisdom and grace.

In Jesus' name, Amen.

Continued Prayers,

Love Me

Pillow Talk

I've often heard the term "pillow talk" those intimate conversations couples have at the end of the day. For a long time, I wasn't sure what that meant for me.

According to the Urban Dictionary, the most common understanding of pillow talk is intimate conversation with a romantic partner in bed, typically after sex. It's a moment when personal thoughts, desires, and worries are shared openly and honestly. The thoughts you keep guarded during the day come to the surface, fully transparent to your partner. Pillow talk can range from playful and silly to deep and serious, but its defining feature is complete candor, no pretenses, just the authentic you.

Like many of you, as a mother, my days were so full that there was hardly any time for pillow talk. When my head hit the pillow, there was no time for conversation; just lights out.

My routine was exhausting: get everyone out the door, work, pick everyone up, fix dinner, help with homework, put out the small fires of the day, get everyone fed, bathed, and even read the Bible to them. By the time my husband and I had a quiet moment, I was too drained to connect. Not to mention sex was obsolete.

On the other hand, my husband was just as drained as I was. He worked all day, came home to spend a few hours with the children, sometimes started dinner himself, took out the trash, fixed whatever was broken in the house, and cut the grass; his list was just as long as mine. Yet, somehow, sex was never off the table. Before long, this imbalance led to arguments over even the simplest things, like finding time for intimacy.

Sometimes finding a babysitter could be a challenge for us or creating a good work life balance. After a few years of marriage, I realized that our marriage needed intentional nurturing. It wasn't just about surviving the day; it was about thriving together. That's when we started exploring what "pillow talk" could really mean not just small talk, but moments to share our hearts, dreams, struggles, and even pray together.

The Bible reminds us:

"Therefore, a man shall leave his father and mother and hold fast to his wife, and they shall become one flesh" Genesis 2:24.

This "oneness" isn't just physical, it's emotional, spiritual, and relational. God calls us to be deeply connected to our spouses, and sometimes that connection begins in the quiet of the night, in the soft whispers on our pillows.

Starting small, we made intentional time at the end of the day. Sometimes it was a few words of gratitude, sometimes prayer together, sometimes simply sharing how we were feeling. Over time, these moments strengthened our bond and reminded us that our marriage is a sacred partnership.

"Let each of you look not only to his own interests, but also to the interests of others" Philippians 2:4.

In marriage, pillow talk becomes a way to look beyond ourselves, to truly care for the heart of our spouse. It's not about perfection, but about intentional connection.

Challenge:

Tonight, before you drift to sleep, set aside even five minutes to talk with your spouse. Share a prayer, a thankfulness, or simply ask about their heart. Watch how God uses those small moments to deepen your intimacy.

Small Things:

Sometimes, building connections in marriage doesn't require grand gestures, it's the small, intentional moments that deepen love and intimacy. These little acts can help you slow down, focus on each other, and invite God into your daily life together.

Ideas for creating sacred moments:

- Move the coffee table aside and dance to your favorite songs. (Ecclesiastes 3:4 – "A time to weep and a time to laugh, a time to mourn and a time to dance.")

- Put the children to bed early and sit together on the porch under the stars. (Psalm 19:1 – "The heavens declare the glory of God; the skies proclaim the work of his hands.")

- Spread a blanket on the living room floor and feed each other grapes. (Song of Solomon 2:3 – "Like an apple tree among the trees of the forest is my beloved among the young men. I delight to sit in his shade…")

- Share a glass of wine while talking about your day. (Ecclesiastes 9:7 – "Go, eat your bread with joy, and drink your wine with a merry heart; for God has already accepted your works.")

- Take a warm bubble bath together, relaxing both body and mind. (1 Corinthians 7:3-4 – "The husband should give to his wife her conjugal rights, and likewise the wife to her husband.")

- End the evening with gentle stretches or exercises together. (1 Corinthians 10:31 – "So whether you eat or drink or whatever you do, do it all for the glory of God.")

These small, mindful moments invite laughter, conversation, and tenderness into your marriage. They remind you that intimacy isn't just about grand gestures, it's about presence, care, and delighting in one another as God intended.

Reflection:_____

Letter to Abba:

Dear Abba Father,

Thank You for the gift of my marriage and for the blessing of my spouse. I am grateful for the time You have given us together and ask that we may never take a single moment for granted.

Help us to cherish each moment, making our time together meaningful and filled with love. Grant us patience when one of us is weary, and help us to notice and consider each other's needs, following Your example of compassion and gentleness.

Teach us to speak life and encouragement over one another, replacing frustration and defensiveness with grace and peace. May we always serve one another in every action and word, reflecting Your love in our marriage.

In Jesus' name, Amen.

Continued Prayers,

Love Me

Tools for maintaining a dating mindset in Marriage

There are several established tools that offer couples healthy roadmaps for staying connected, but the most important foundation for maintaining a *dating mindset* in marriage is a shared commitment to growth both individually and collectively.

It is often said, *"The same things you did to get your spouse are the same things you must continue to do to keep them."* While simple, this statement holds a great deal of truth. Marriage was never meant to be placed on autopilot. Scripture reminds us, *"Let us not be weary in well doing: for in due season, we shall reap, if we faint not"* (Galatians 6:9, KJV). Love requires intentional effort over time.

The reality is that none of us remain the same. As individuals, we are either growing or declining, never standing still. As seasons change, so do we. The interests, dreams, and rhythms of life we embraced in our twenties may look very different in our sixties. *"To everything there is a season, and a time to every purpose under the heaven"* (Ecclesiastes 3:1, KJV).

So how do couples navigate these changing waters together? The answer begins with choosing curiosity over assumption and commitment over comfort. Dating in marriage means continually learning your spouse's heart, just as you once did. Scripture encourages this posture of love: *"Be kindly affectioned one to another with brotherly love; in honor preferring one another"* (Romans 12:10, KJV).

A dating mindset in marriage reflects Christlike love, patient, attentive, and growing. *"Charity suffereth long, and is kind… seeketh not her own"* (1 Corinthians 13:4–5, KJV). When couples commit to growing together, honoring each season, and pursuing one another with intention, their marriage remains alive, green, and flourishing.

The Greats….

Some of the tools commonly used in the field of Marriage and Family are listed below. You may recognize a few of them, while others may be new to you. While these tools can be helpful, they are not the only solution. Ultimately, each couple is encouraged to seek God for wisdom and guidance; asking Him to reveal ways to strengthen their marriage, renew their perspective of one another, and keep their relationship fresh. When couples invite God into the process, He provides simple yet meaningful ways to maintain a dating mindset and continue growing together.

Gottman Relationship Checkup

The Gottman Relationship Checkup is a research-based online assessment developed by Drs. John and Julie Gottman to evaluate the health of a couple's relationship across key domains. This assessment emphasizes team building by highlighting areas of growth in a relationship.

<u>Dr. Gary Chapman- Love Language Assessment.</u>

The Love Languages assessment was created by Dr. Gary Chapman and is widely recognized in the field of relationships. He introduced it in his book *The 5 Love Languages: How to Express Heartfelt Commitment to Your Mate*, first published in 1992. The assessment is commonly used in marriage counseling, relationship education, and personal development to help couples understand and meet each other's emotional needs.

The assessment identifies a person's primary "love language" from the following five categories:

1. Words of Affirmation
2. Acts of Service
3. Receiving Gifts
4. Quality Time

5. Physical Touch

Gottman & Sullaway – CCQ (Couples Communication Questionnaire)

A very common couples communication assessment is the Communication Patterns Questionnaire (CPQ). It was originally developed to assess how couples communicate during conflict and everyday interactions. It was created by John M. Gottman and Neil Sullaway (1984) with further work by Andrew Christensen and colleagues in the late 1980s and 1990s.

Stephen Kendrick and Alex Kendrick Love Dare

It was first published in 2008 and is a 40-day devotional designed to help couples strengthen their marriage through daily challenges, reflection, and intentional acts of love. The Kendricks are filmmakers and authors known for their work on faith-based marriage and family resources.

Greg & Julie Gorman- Married for a Purpose

The Gorman's have written several books including a 52-week devotional that helps couples form new habits of thinking for a higher way of living. They have dedicated their work to helping couples live with purpose focused over problem focused.

Drs. Les & Leslie Parrott- SYMBIS (Saving your Marriage Before it Starts)

SYMBIS stands for *Saving Your Marriage Before It Starts*. It's a research-based relationship assessment designed to help couples understand themselves and each other more deeply as they prepare for marriage or seek to strengthen their existing marriage. It is not just a test, but a tool paired with guided discussion to create meaningful insight and growth.

There are many tools and resources available that help couples maintain the flame of love in their marriage or resolve unnecessary conflicts. But it is essential to discern which tools work best for your unique relationship. Scripture reminds us, *"Iron sharpeneth iron; so, a man sharpeneth the countenance of his friend"* (Proverbs 27:17, KJV). Just as we seek guidance and wisdom in other areas of life, it is wise to seek help when needed in marriage.

There is nothing wrong with asking for professional guidance. God encourages us to grow, learn, and work diligently in every part of life. *"And whatsoever ye do, do it heartily, as to the Lord, and not unto men"* (Colossians 3:23, KJV). Marriage is worth the effort we invest because it is a reflection of God's love and faithfulness. Commit to intentionally nurturing your relationship, applying the tools God leads you to, and trusting Him to guide your hearts closer together. *"Two are better than one; because they have a good reward for their labour. For if they fall, the one will lift up his fellow"* (Ecclesiastes 4:9-10, KJV).

Reflection:

_____

_____

_____

_____

_____

_____

_____

_____

_____

_____

_____

_____

_____

_____

_____

_____

_____

––––––––––––––––––––––––––––––––

––––––––––––––––––––––––––––––––

Letter to Abba

Dear Abba Father,

We come to You asking for guidance in caring for our marriage. Please show us the tools and wisdom we need to grow together, resolve conflicts in love, and keep our relationship vibrant. Help us to seek You first in every decision, and teach us to reflect Your love in all that we do together. Lord, remind us that there is nothing wrong with seeking guidance when we need it, and that the things truly worth having in life are the things we are willing to work hard for.

Help us to grow together and not apart. Teach us to love with intention, to remain curious about one another, and to honor every season of our marriage. Renew our hearts, Lord, so that our love continues to reflect Your grace, patience, and faithfulness.

We ask this in Jesus' name, **Amen.**

Continued Prayers,

Love Me

Love Map

I remember during a *Muscles for Marriage* call, Abba Father gently reminded me of something important: sometimes I assume I know how to pray for my husband or what his day will look like. I might even say, "I prayed for him today," without asking what he actually needs prayer for or what his priorities are.

This isn't usually done out of neglect or lack of love, it's often the result of comfort. After being with someone for a while, it's easy to think we already know their needs, their struggles, or their plans. But God calls us to love intentionally, which includes praying with purpose and understanding.

Have you ever found yourself doing this, mapping out your spouse's day in your mind and assuming you know what they need?

Take a moment to consider: Are you praying out of assumption or intentionality? Are you actively seeking your spouse's heart, or simply going on autopilot?

Create a Love Map Together

1. Take two pens, a notebook, and your Bible. Ask your spouse to do the same.

2. Write down the things that stand out as your spouse shares. These notes will guide your prayers and help you understand their heart more deeply.

Creating a Love Map exercise is a practical way for couples to deepen intimacy and understanding. Love Maps are part of Dr. John Gottman's research on building strong marriages, they involve knowing your partner's inner world: thoughts, feelings, stresses, and dreams. Here's a step-by-step guide you can follow:

Step 1: Set the Intention

- Choose a quiet time without distractions.

- Decide that the goal is curiosity and connection, not judgment.
- Remind yourselves that this is a safe space to share and listen.

Step 2: Prepare Questions

Gottman emphasizes learning the "small stuff" about your partner. Use open-ended questions in categories like:

Daily Life & Routine

- What is your partner's favorite way to spend a day off?
- What is their current favorite food, TV show, or hobby?

Stress & Challenges

- What stresses them out at work or school?
- How do they usually respond to challenges or conflict?

Emotions & Inner World

- What worries them the most right now?
- What are they excited about or looking forward to?

Dreams & Goals

- What are their short-term and long-term dreams?
- What are some personal goals they've never shared?

Step 3: Take Turns Asking and Listening

- One partner asks a question while the other answers.
- Listen actively, don't interrupt or correct.
- Show interest with follow-up questions or affirmations like, "Tell me more about that."

Step 4: Take Notes

- Write down key points in a notebook or journal.

- This helps you remember important details and track changes over time.

- Treat it like updating a "mental map" of your partner's world.

Step 5: Reflect and Share

- Discuss what surprised you or what you learned.

- Talk about ways you can support your partner better.

- Highlight moments of gratitude for your partner's qualities.

Step 6: Make It a Habit

- Schedule a regular "Love Map check-in" weekly or monthly.

- Revisit and update the map as life circumstances and preferences change.

Optional Variation

- Love Map Cards: Write questions on cards and take turns picking one.
- Themed Maps: Focus on specific areas like finances, dreams, intimacy, or stress.

Reflection:

_____

_____

_____

_____

_____

_____

_____

_____

_____

_____

_____

_____

_____

_____

_____

_____

_____

_____

After creating your Love Map, create your prayer as a couple.

Letter to Abba

Dear Abba Father,

_____

_____

_____

_____

_____

_____

_____

_____

_____

_____

_____

_____

We ask this in Jesus' name,

Amen.

Continued Prayers,

Love Us

The SUM

If I had to sum up marriage in one word, it would be: *change*. Would you agree? I often think back to 1999, when my husband and I said, "I do." Life felt so different then.

Most weddings back then took place in a church, a cozy living room, or a serene park. Friends, family, and neighbors often had opinions about whether the couple would last. In small towns especially, weddings were a big deal, sometimes even making the local newspaper. Announcements of these life milestones were published with the same care as other important news, marking the beginning of a new chapter for the couple.

All the talk and opinions from others often stirred anxiety and doubt, prompting questions like, *"Am I making the right choice? Can we really make this work? Are they truly my person?"*

The chatter wasn't random; it was tied to many factors. People commented on the couple's age, family connections, church affiliation, and even socioeconomic status. While these external opinions could feel overwhelming, the sum is that it reminded couples that marriage is ultimately about trusting God's guidance above the world's expectations.

Statistics

I recently read an article stating that many young adults today are choosing to delay or even opt out of marriage, often due to fears of divorce or the belief that cohabitation is a simpler path. In fact, the CDC reports that over 56% of Americans over the age of 18 believe living together is easier than marriage. Looking back, about 2.25 million couples were married in 1999, a striking reminder of how much has changed. While society's views may shift, God's design for marriage remains a foundation for love, commitment, and growth, guiding couples through every season and challenge.

Fast forward to 2024, and the CDC reports that approximately 2,390,482 marriages took place in the United States. While the numbers have shifted slightly, one thing remains the same: every marriage is a journey of change. From young love to shared dreams, from challenges to celebrations, the seasons of marriage call us to grow together and with God.

Shifting

Although change can be hard, it also reminds us that we are not the same people we were on our wedding day and that is a beautiful thing. Each chapter invites us to lean on God's guidance, strengthen our love, and embrace the evolving story He is writing in our hearts.

Whether we realize it or not, change always causes a reaction within us. How we respond often depends on where the change occurs in our lives and how deeply it touches us. Many of us struggle with change, it can feel uncomfortable or even overwhelming, but as we've already noted, change is inevitable.

The key is not to resist it, but to trust that God can use every shift, every new season, to shape us, strengthen us, and draw us closer to one another and to Him.

Stress is the body's natural response to substantial or unusual demands whether physical, environmental, or interpersonal. For couples, stress can arise from busy schedules, financial pressures, family responsibilities, or even miscommunication. It often shows up as irritability, anxiety, tension, or even physical symptoms like high blood pressure.

But stress is not meant to control us. Scripture reminds us:

"Cast all your anxiety on him because he cares for you" 1 Peter 5:7.

Stress is less a fixed state of being and more a process, a signal that something in our lives needs attention. As partners, we can support one another by listening, praying together, and seeking God's guidance in the midst of challenges.

"Therefore, encourage one another and build each other up, just as in fact you are doing" 1 Thessalonians 5:11.

Marriage is a journey where stress will come and go, but God calls us to face it together, leaning on Him and one another. When we do, we not only survive stress we grow stronger, closer, and more resilient in love. Our marriages can serve as a living example to those who have delayed or chosen to opt out of marriage, showing the truth of Scripture:

"Two are better than one, because they have a good return for their labor" Ecclesiastes 4:9.

Don't allow stress to overwhelm you. Bring your worries and burdens to the feet of Jesus, trusting Him to carry what is too heavy for you. When we surrender our stress to God, He replaces it with peace, enabling us to live the productive, fulfilling, and promising life He has planned for us.

"Come to me, all you who are weary and burdened, and I will give you rest. Take my yoke upon you and learn from me, for I am gentle and humble in heart, and you will find rest for your souls. For my yoke is easy and my burden is light," Matthew 11:28-30.

Reflection:

_____

_____

_____

_____

_____

_____

_____

_____

_____

_____

_____

_____

_____

_____

_____

_____

_____

_____

_____

Letter to Abba

Dear Abba Father,

Thank You for guarding my heart and mind, and for not allowing me to be distracted by the voices or opinions of others. Thank You for keeping me focused on the beautiful promises You have spoken over my life and my marriage.

Thank You for the gentle reminders found in Your Word, reminders of the good plans You have prepared for me. Thank You that I may come boldly before Your altar to receive mercy, grace, and help in every season.

I am deeply grateful that You have chosen my marriage as a reflection of Your Kingdom on the earth. Thank You that every negative word spoken against it has been cast aside and holds no power over my destiny.

Thank You for knowing me even before I was formed in my mother's womb. You are a mighty God; all-knowing and all-wise. I rejoice that I can call You Abba Father, confident that You hear my prayers and faithfully answer when I call.

Thank You, Abba, for loving me so completely and so well.

Amen.

Continued Prayers,

Love Me

The Atmosphere

Babies bring an indescribable joy to the heart. When I think about rocking a baby, I'm reminded of how calming the experience is, the gentle rhythm, the soft scent of a newborn, and the comfort they bring as they rest on your chest without a care in the world. There is something about babies that invites nearly everyone to see life through a new lens. If you aren't careful, you may find yourself simply watching them sleep, filled with quiet admiration.

I remember when I had my first son, my grandmother was beyond excited to meet her first great-grandson. When he was about two months old, I went to visit her and brought along all the outfits I thought she would love: bibbed overalls, little suits, jean outfits, and more. She was absolutely delighted. She told all of her friends what he was wearing and how adorable he was. My heart overflowed with joy, because simply holding my baby seemed to bring my grandmother's laughter fully to life.

I'm also reminded of the time I volunteered with a ministry that visited nursing homes to deliver personal hygiene items to seniors. Whenever children came with us, the atmosphere completely changed. Faces that were once quiet and still began to light up. Even those who hadn't smiled would soften at the sight of a small child. I couldn't help but ask myself: what is it about children that bring such joy and warmth to so many hearts?

The answer is truly simple; children are a gift from God. Scripture reminds us, *"Children are a heritage from the Lord, offspring a reward from Him"* (Psalm 127:3). Their presence naturally brings joy, peace, and light into a room. But this truth invites a deeper question for each of us: what happens when we walk into a room?

As believers, we are called to carry more than our personalities or moods, we are meant to carry the peace of God. The Bible tells us, *"And let the peace of God rule in your hearts"* (Colossians 3:15). When we enter a space, does the atmosphere shift toward peace, encouragement, and love? Or does it grow heavy with tension, criticism, or unrest?

Scripture reminds us that our presence matters. *"Blessed are the peacemakers, for they shall be called the children of God"* (Matthew 5:9). Just as children naturally bring joy, we are called to intentionally bring peace. The Holy Spirit within us should influence the environment around us for the better.

When people see us coming, may they not feel dread or discomfort, but hope and reassurance. May our words build up, our attitudes reflect Christ, and our presence invite God's peace. *"Let your light so shine before men, that they may see your good works and glorify your Father which is in heaven"* (Matthew 5:16).

Many of us expect others to change the atmosphere for us or make it better....but is that truly a realistic expectation?

Hard Truth

In many cases, people struggle to create peaceful and loving environments because they were never shown what that looks like. When someone has grown up in toxic or broken surroundings, peace can feel unfamiliar, even uncomfortable. Scripture reminds us, *"Train up a child in the way he should go"* (Proverbs 22:6). What we are trained in, whether healthy or harmful, often shapes how we respond to others later in life.

It is easy to expect people to stand up for us or advocate on our behalf. Yet many have never learned how to advocate for themselves. How can someone give what they have never received? *"Can the blind lead the blind? Will they not both fall into a pit?"* (Luke 6:39). Without guidance, understanding, and healing, it becomes difficult to lead, protect, or support others well.

The unfortunate truth is that it can take time to recognize these patterns. In the process, we may miss opportunities for deeper connection, growth, and peace. But God is patient with us. *"He heals the brokenhearted and binds up their wounds"* (Psalm 147:3). What we did not learn early in life, God can lovingly teach us through His Word and His Spirit.

Through Christ, we are not bound by our past environments. *"If anyone is in Christ, he is a new creation"* (2 Corinthians 5:17). God invites us into healing, showing us how to cultivate peace, love, and courage, first within ourselves, and then in the lives of others. While our paths to peace may differ, marriage invites us to pursue serenity with intention. As we seek God together, He meets us in those quiet places, nurturing peace within our hearts and our relationship.

Reflection:

_____

_____

_____

_____

_____

_____

_____

_____

_____

_____

_____

_____

_____

_____

_____

_____

_____

A Letter to Abba

Dear Abba,

Lord, help me recognize the areas in my life where healing is still needed. Teach me how to create peace where I once knew pain and guide me as I learn to stand firm in Your truth. Restore what was missed and help me walk forward in wholeness. Lord, help me to be mindful of the atmosphere I carry. Let Your peace go before me, Your love surrounds me, and Your presence be felt through my words and actions. May I reflect You in every room I enter, impacting all others to surrender to Your will and Your way. In Jesus Name!

We ask this in Jesus' name,

Amen.

Continued Prayers,

Love Me

In-L-O-V-E-S

Most of us have heard the stories or lived them, about the challenges that can come with in-law relationships. I remember a friend who, shortly after getting married, described learning how to navigate life with in-laws as a complete nightmare. It raises an honest question many married couples face: *How do we honor the relationship with the one we love while wisely navigating the waters of extended family?*

Even the term *"in-law"* can feel distant, almost transactional, as though it describes a relationship bound more by obligation than by love. Yet Scripture gives us a deeper lens.

In Biblical Hebrew, there is no single generic term for "in-law." Instead, specific words are used to describe each relationship. One set uses cham for "father-in-law" and chamot for "mother-in-law." Another uses choten and chotenet for the same roles. Scripture applies these words across different family stories In Exodus 18, Moses and his father-in-law Jethro, Judah and Tamar, Ruth and Naomi, each revealing the real tensions, complexities, and growth that come when families are joined together.

These accounts remind us that blending families has *always* required patience, humility, and grace. The Bible does not hide the challenges, but it consistently points us toward love as the solution.

Jesus Himself said He did not come to abolish the law, but to fulfill it. And how did He fulfill it? Through love. His love led Him to the cross, and throughout Scripture He continually emphasizes how central love is to life in God's Kingdom.

For married couples today, this truth still stands. Love is not only meant to bind husband and wife, but to shape how we relate to those who come with our marriage. When love leads rooted in Christ; it creates room for wisdom, boundaries, forgiveness, and peace, even in the most difficult family dynamics.

Some of this I did not understand at first, because no one really teaches us that no matter where we sit at the table, whether as a new son- or daughter-in-love, or as parents on either side, the transition can feel uncomfortable for everyone involved.

I remember the challenges I faced with my own mother-in-love. I married her only child, and that alone brought its own set of adjustments. Some of our struggles were shaped by life experiences, others by simple misunderstandings, and still others by stubborn habits neither of us knew how to release at the time. Because of those experiences, I began praying early, long before my children were old enough to marry, that I would one day be a blessing to my own daughters-in-love, both at the beginning of their marriages and throughout the years that followed. In His faithfulness, God gave me the tools and wisdom to navigate those relationships by offering me a deeper glimpse into His own relationship with us, one marked by patience, grace, and enduring love.

Allowing our children to grow into the responsible adults we have trained them to be requires a deep act of trust. It means trusting their ability to choose the spouse God has given them to walk through life with and allowing that spouse to be fully who God created them to be as they build a life together. While there may be moments when we think we would have done things differently, loving our children well means giving young couples the space to make decisions for their own family and supporting them as they do. Guidance has its place, but trust and encouragement are key to helping their marriage flourish.

Haven't we all wanted to try something on our own, even when others offered what they believed was a better way? Most of us have. In the same way, God does not dictate every detail of our choices. He doesn't tell us what color bike to ride, but when we fall, He is always there to help us back up. Sometimes we must walk through a trial more than once before wisdom takes root. There is no perfect outline for what *"in-loves"* should or should not do. Family dynamics are deeply personal, shaped by history, culture, and individual personalities. Yet one important truth remains: everyone has a rightful place, and God is intentional about order within families.

Marriage creates a new covenant. Scripture reminds us that a husband and wife are called to leave, cleave, and become one not to abandon family, but to establish a new foundation rooted in unity.

"Therefore, a man shall leave his father and his mother and hold fast to his wife, and they shall become one flesh." **Genesis 2:24**

This new union does not erase the value of parents or extended family; instead, it clarifies roles. Parents are called to support, encourage, and release, while couples are called to lead their household with wisdom and love.

"For God is not a God of confusion but of peace." **1 Corinthians 14:33**

When each person honors their God-given place, peace has room to grow. Boundaries become an act of love, not rejection. Respect replaces control, and trust replaces fear.

Above all, love must be the guiding principle in every relationship. Love covers misunderstandings, softens difficult conversations, and strengthens unity within marriage and family.

"Above all, love each other deeply, because love covers over a multitude of sins." **1 Peter 4:8**

As couples navigate relationships with in-loves, wisdom comes through humility, prayer, and grace remembering that God is at work in every generation.

"Trust in the Lord with all your heart... and He will make your paths straight." Proverbs 3:5–6

Reflection:

_____

_____

_____

_____

_____

_____

_____

_____

_____

_____

_____

_____

_____

A Letter to Abba

Dear Abba,

I enter Your courts with praise and thanksgiving. Thank You for teaching me how to love my family and for showing me how the love of Christ guides my words, my actions, and even my heart as I respond to my in-loves today.

Lord, teach me to love as You love. Grant me wisdom to navigate family relationships with grace, patience, and humility. May my marriage reflect Your love in every relationship we hold. Help me to be slow to speak and quick to listen. Teach me when to respond with wisdom and when to simply smile and trust You.

Lead me into the quiet, peaceful places where I can walk closely with You. Give me discernment in how to pray for my in-loves as they navigate the seasons of their lives. Help us to place all things in proper order, according to

Your will. May we dwell together in unity and
love, bringing glory to You in all we do.

We ask this in Jesus' name,

Amen.

Continued Prayers,

Love Me

Special Prayer

Abba Father,

I thank You for every couple who has taken the time to read and reflect on this devotional. I pray Your abundant blessings over their lives and their marriage. May their union continue to thrive and prosper in every area, spiritually, emotionally, physically, and financially. Let their marriage be a living testimony of Your love, so that others clearly see You at work in their union. Strengthen their ministry together and draw them into deeper intimacy with You and with one another.

I pray that You would supply more than enough for every need, empowering them to fulfill Your will and purpose for their lives. May this devotional have searched the deep places of their hearts, sparked meaningful conversations, and brought greater understanding, unity, and peace into their marriage.

We place all of this in Your loving hands. In Jesus' name, Amen.

www.ingramcontent.com/pod-product-compliance
Lightning Source LLC
Chambersburg PA
CBHW061045110426
42740CB00049B/2190